The New Job Interview Workbook

Turning your opportunity into a job offer

by Ray Blake

INTRODUCTION	5
WHAT WILL HAPPEN AT THE INTERVIEW?	7
Part 1: Introductions and rapport	7
Part 2: Structured questioning	8
Part 3: Your questions and next steps	9
PREPARING FOR THE INTERVIEW	13
Rapport questions	13
Structured questioning	18
Management	32
Your questions and next steps	44

Introduction

You've been invited to a job interview, or perhaps you're hoping to get invited to one soon.

Has it been a while since you had a job interview? Maybe this will be your first job interview. Often, the mere thought of having to attend one can be terrifying. After all, there's so much at stake. This might be the job of your dreams, or it might be the job you need to keep your household functioning. Either way, a lot can hang on this interview.

But there's good news. When you are called to an interview it is because THEY WANT TO GIVE YOU THE JOB.

That seems an odd thing to say, doesn't it? Why don't they just give you the job if that's the case? Why are they putting you and however many other poor saps through this ordeal? Well, let me explain…

The early stages of the recruitment process are all about filtering people out, getting rid of applicants they don't think can do the job. Out go the application forms completed in crayon. Out go the ones that arrive without the requested references and the other ones with obvious gross errors.

Then someone will sit down with the remaining applications. They'll check the details. Are the noted qualifications what they asked for? Does this person have the required experience? Do they sound like they'd be a good fit for this vacancy? These are questions aimed at eliminating candidates so they are left with a shortlist (literally, a short list) of people to interview.

Right up to the point of finalising the shortlist, the process has been about finding reasons NOT to hire applicants, weeding out the people they DON'T want. But the shortlist is composed entirely of people with the right experience, the right qualifications and who look like they're made of the right stuff. They would be happy to take on any of these people, subject to a good interview. In fact, they WANT to hire at least one of the people on that list and in most cases they will. The interview therefore is not about getting rid of people. They are not looking for reasons NOT to hire you; THEY ARE LOOKING FOR REASONS TO SAY YES.

That interview you are attending is an event for you to show the people who want to give you a job that they're right to want to give you a job. With just a little preparation, you can make it an easy and enjoyable experience. This workbook will take you through the whole process of preparing.

What will happen at the interview?

If you are faced with a good interviewer (and you probably will be), there should be three distinct phases to the interview:

1. Introductions and rapport
2. Structured questioning
3. Your questions and next steps

Part 1: Introductions and rapport

The interviewer's first job is to effect introductions and put you at your ease. The questions he/she will later be asking you might be quite direct and probing, so he/she will want to develop a rapport first that will make asking those questions seem a little less intrusive or blunt.

A handshake should accompany the introduction. Unless you know the interviewer, do not expect nor offer a kiss or hug. I won't waste time talking about handshaking technique. You know how to shake hands; let's not over-think it.

Your interviewer will ask you some questions to get you talking. There are some standard ones, and in this workbook we'll prepare draft answers to all of them. You might be asked what you know about the company, or you might be asked about hobbies and interests you noted in your application or your cv/resume.

The questions you are asked will be open ones; you won't be able to answer with a simple yes or no. They will force you to answer with sentences or paragraphs.

Part 2: Structured questioning

This will be the longest part of the interview. Your interviewer will have a list of questions (either on paper or in their head) that are designed to get a deep insight into your skills, your experience and your approach to work.

If your interviewer knows what he or she is doing, most of the questions here will begin with, "Tell me about a time when you…" rather than, "How would you deal with…" The reason is that the first format requires you to give examples of things you have actually done in real situations, whilst the second allows you to use conjecture and imagination and won't necessarily be a reliable guide to how you are likely to behave when working at the interviewer's business.

Even if your interviewer doesn't know about this technique, make sure you prepare for it and that when you answer the "How would you deal with…" questions, you turn them around yourself and answer with, "Well, when this happened to me in my last position, what I did was…"

A good interviewer will probe and test your answers. They will ask for more detail sometimes.

If you're describing a situation where you got a good result, they may ask follow-up questions like:

> *What difficulties did you encounter?*
>
> *How did you overcome them?*
>
> *What happened after you finished?*
>
> *And what is the situation there like now?*

This can sound like they're trying to catch you out. They're not. Remember, they think you can do this job. They want to hire you. They just need a little more evidence to reassure them that they're right. Give it to them.

Part 3: Your questions and next steps

At the end of the interview, your interviewer will ask you if you have any questions to ask. You should ask at least one question, but no more than two. The interviewer will only have allocated a minute or two for this stage and you don't want to be the cause of them running late.

The last thing you want is to suddenly realise you can't think of a question to ask when they offer you the opportunity. That's why in this workbook we will prepare a few questions from which you will select when the time comes.

If you have lots of questions, you might want to tell your interviewer that and offer to follow up with them by phone or email if time is short now.

When he or she has answered your questions, it will be time to end the discussion, and this will normally be by way of the interviewer outlining the next steps. It would be rare to be offered the job on the spot. More likely would be a promise to follow up with you by phone or letter within a given time frame.

Then it's time to stand up, shake hands again and make your way out. You have two final things to say at this point. The first is something like, "Thank you for your time today." The second is this:

> *Will there be an opportunity to receive feedback on my interview performance?*

Partly, of course, you're saying this because it will impress the hell out of the interviewer. But actually, you really want that feedback. Whether you get this job or not, you will probably be sitting in another interview seat at some time in the future, and based on feedback you get now you can improve your performance (and thus your employability) next time. You want to know what they liked about your answers and what they didn't, what they might have preferred to have heard. In all likelihood, if you've prepared along the lines outlined in this workbook, they'll like way more than they don't.

Preparing for the interview

At this point, you should grab a pen and start recording your thoughts in this book. Or, in a separate notebook write down the questions you'll read and then jot down your answers. It's probably best if you just jot down bullet points rather than trying to write in proper sentences. Later, you can practice turning these bullet points into a coherent spoken answer. If you need to flesh out your notes you can do so then.

Rapport questions

The rapport questions you may face are likely to be about either the company or your interests. Prepare to answer either or both.

So, what do you know about this company/service?

Research online so you can show a basic understanding of the organisation you are hoping to join.

If it's a business, find out the following and note down your answers:

How long have they been in business?

What are their main products or services?

What are their main markets (e.g. retail or wholesale, local or international, mass-market or luxury)?

If it is not a business, but a service like a school or hospital, research the following:

How long have they been running?

What are their specialisms?

What awards or accolades have they recently earned?

Don't feel you have to share everything you've learned about the organisation. Your interviewer will expect only a couple of sentences with maybe 4 or 5 key facts. Don't spend more than a minute answering the "What do you know about" question.

So, I see you are interested in ... Tell me about that.

If asked like this, your job is to give them enough to answer the question, but not so much that you'll bore them to tears. Practice an approach based on the following prompts to fill about 30 seconds to a minute. If the interviewer wants to hear more than that, let them ask you a follow-up question.

How long have you had this interest?

What first attracted you to this interest?

When do you devote time to it and how much?

What do you enjoy about it?

How do you hope to continue – or move to the next level?

Possible follow-up questions will build on those listed above. Here are some you might prepare some thoughts on:

What's the most important piece of advice you'd give to someone wanting to start doing this?

Who have you introduced to this interest and how have they got on with it?

What does/do your spouse/partner/friends think about your interest?

Structured questioning

You will probably only get asked a few of these questions, but you won't know which ahead of time. So you need to prepare for each of them, as well as any obvious follow-up questions. In each case, I've given you space to answer the lead question and some follow-ups, but based on your answer other follow-ups may suggest themselves, so note these and answer them as they occur to you.

Some key points to observe:

- Use 'I' statements, not 'we' statements. The interviewer will want to know what your role was.
- Don't exaggerate your own involvement in past projects. If you were part of a team, say so. Specify exactly what your role and responsibilities were. A good interviewer will probe for this detail in any event.
- On the day, if you're not sure what the interviewer is asking, ask for clarification.

Before you get to the questions, though, it is worth spending some time with the job specification and other papers you have been sent. Using the questions overleaf, try and isolate in your notes in your own words what the organisation is looking for in a candidate for this role.

What do they want to see in a candidate?

What aspects of my part work or other experience will be most relevant?

Use the answer to this second question when working through the preparation in the pages that follow.

Lead question:
Tell me about a time when you had to work as part of a team.

Which job was this? If not a job, where was it – e.g. school, church, sports team?

What was the situation? What were you trying to achieve?

What was your role in the team?

What was the outcome and how did your efforts contribute to the result?

Follow-up questions

What difficulties did you encounter?

How did you overcome them?

What happened after you finished?

And what is the situation there like now?

With this and each lead question that follows, think about other possible questions that may come up. Note them down in your notebook and answer them.

**Lead question:
Tell me about a time when you had to pay attention to quality.**

Which job was this? If not a job, where was it – e.g. school, church, sports team?

What was the situation? What were you trying to achieve?

Why was quality so important? What would have happened in the absence of quality?

What quality measures did you use?

What was the outcome?

Follow-up questions

What difficulties did you encounter?

How did you overcome them?

What happened after you finished?

And what is the situation there like now?

Lead question:
Tell me about a time when you had to work under time pressure.

Which job was this? If not a job, where was it – e.g. school, church, sports team?

What was the situation? What were you trying to achieve?

Why was there pressure on time? What would have happened if it had come in late?

How did you make sure you met the deadlines?

Follow-up questions

What difficulties did you encounter?

How did you overcome them?

What happened after you finished?

And what is the situation there like now?

The New Job Interview Workbook

**Lead question:
Tell me about a time when you had to handle a customer complaint.**

Which job was this? If not a job, where was it – e.g. school, church, sports team?

What was the complaint about? Was it justified?

How did you address the complaint?

How did you make sure the customer felt they had been treated fairly?

Follow-up questions

What difficulties did you encounter?

How did you overcome them?

What was the customer's attitude in the end?

Lead question:
Tell me about a time when you had to persuade someone to do something.

Which job was this? If not a job, where was it – e.g. school, church, sports team?

What was the situation? What were you trying to achieve?

What approaches did you consider and what did you use?

How well did that work?

What was the outcome?

Follow-up questions

What difficulties did you encounter? What objections were raised?

How did you overcome them?

What happened after you finished?

And what is the situation there like now?

Lead question:
Tell me about a time when you had to make a presentation.

Which job was this? If not a job, where was it – e.g. school, church, sports team?

What was the presentation about? Who were your audience?

How did you prepare?

How did it go on the day?

Follow-up questions

What difficulties did you encounter?

How did you overcome them?

What questions did people ask and how did you respond?

What happened after the presentation?

Management

The remainder of the questions in this section are most relevant for management roles.

If there is some expectation that the job for which you have applied will require you to undertake some sort of leadership or management element, you should consider working through these sections even if it is not primarily a management role.

**Lead question:
Tell me about a time when you had to appraise a team member's performance.**

Which job was this? If not a job, where was it – e.g. school, church, sports team?

Who did you have to appraise?

How did you prepare?

How did you discuss the appraisal with them?

What was the outcome?

Follow-up questions

What difficulties did you encounter?

How did you overcome them?

What if anything have you done differently more recently as a result of this experience?

Lead question:
Tell me about a time where you had to deal with an underperformance issue.

Which job was this? If not a job, where was it – e.g. school, church, sports team?

What was the underperformance issue?

What did you do about it?

How did you track improvement?

What was the outcome?

Follow-up questions

What difficulties did you encounter?

How did you overcome them?

What if anything have you done differently more recently as a result of this experience?

**Lead question:
Tell me about a time where you had to change your management style to get a result.**

Which job was this? If not a job, where was it – e.g. school, church, sports team?

What was the situation?

Why would your normal management style not have been appropriate?

What did you do differently?

What was the outcome?

Follow-up questions

What difficulties did you encounter?

How did you overcome them?

What if anything have you done differently more recently as a result of this experience?

Lead question:
Tell me about a time where you had to deal with an angry team member.

Which job was this? If not a job, where was it – e.g. school, church, sports team?

Who was angry and why? Were they justified?

How did you try to calm the situation in the short term and mitigate any danger?

How did you approach a longer term remedy?

What was the outcome?

Follow-up questions

What difficulties did you encounter?

How did you overcome them?

What if anything have you done differently more recently as a result of this experience?

Lead question:
Tell me about a time where you had to deliver bad news.

Which job was this? If not a job, where was it – e.g. school, church, sports team?

What news did you have to give and to whom?

Why was this bad news and what did you fear the impact could have been if not handled well?

How did you prepare?

How did you deliver the bad news?

What was the outcome?

Follow-up questions

What difficulties did you encounter?

How did you overcome them?

What if anything have you done differently more recently as a result of this experience?

Lead question:
Tell me about a time where you had to train or coach a team member.

Which job was this? If not a job, where was it – e.g. school, church, sports team?

Who did you have to train or coach? What did they have to learn to do?

How did you prepare?

How did you deliver the coaching or training?

How did you assess their ability when they started to apply the learning?

How did you make sure they continued to develop?

Follow-up questions

What difficulties did you encounter?

How did you overcome them?

What if anything have you done differently more recently as a result of this experience?

Your questions and next steps

You will score points for asking relevant questions. Have several prepared.

Ask only one or two at the interview. If you have a whole list of questions to ask, tell your interviewer that and offer to follow up with them by phone or email if time is short now.

Don't ask a question that has already been covered in the interview process (have some spares just in case!)

Don't rely on your memory for these. Either have this book with you at the interview or transcribe the questions onto an index card. When asked if you have any questions, make a show of consulting your notes. You will earn points for having prepared so diligently.

Here are some questions you might want to ask your interviewer:

- What training can I expect to receive when I start and over the months that follow?
- How often will my performance be appraised and how will I get feedback on my performance in the role?
- What opportunities might there be to travel or work in other locations?
- What has been YOUR experience of working for this organisation?

Note your own questions below.

Remember, at the very end

- Thank you for your time today.
- Will there be an opportunity to receive feedback on my interview performance?

Before you travel to the interview, remember this:

- They want to give you the job
- They already think you can do it
- They are looking for reasons to say yes

Now, go and get your job.

www.ingramcontent.com/pod-product-compliance
Lightning Source LLC
Chambersburg PA
CBHW061229180526
45170CB00003B/1224